E C O N ... E S

D0526205

Privatization in Transition Countries

Lessons of the First Decade

Oleh Havrylyshyn
Donal McGettigan

INTERNATIONAL MONETARY FUND
WASHINGTON, D.C.

©1999 International Monetary Fund

Series Editor
J.R. Morrison
IMF External Relations Department

Cover design and composition
Massoud Etemadi, Choon Lee, and
the IMF Graphics Section

ISBN 1-55775-831-X
ISSN 1020-5098

Published August 1999

To order IMF publications, please contact:

International Monetary Fund, Publication Services
700 19th Street, N.W., Washington, D.C. 20431, U.S.A.
Tel: (202) 623-7430   Telefax: (202) 623-7201
E-mail: publications@imf.org
Internet: http://www.imf.org

Preface

The Economic Issues series aims to make available to a broad readership of nonspecialists some of the economic research being produced on topical issues by IMF staff. The series draws mainly from IMF Working Papers, which are technical papers produced by IMF staff members and visiting scholars, as well as from policy-related research papers.

This Economic Issue draws on material originally contained in IMF Working Paper WP/99/6, "Privatization in Transition Countries: A Sampling of the Literature," by Oleh Havrylyshyn and Donal McGettigan. This version was prepared by Charles S. Gardner; it also appears on the IMF's website (http://www.imf.org). Readers may purchase the Working Paper ($7.00) from IMF Publication Services, or view the latter in full text on the IMF's website.

Privatization in Transition Countries: Lessons of the First Decade

A decade ago, with the breakup of the Soviet Union and the start of market-oriented reforms in many former socialist economies of Central and Eastern Europe, the prospect of privatizing inefficient state-owned companies figured prominently in both popular and academic writings. As the headline event symbolizing change from central planning to capitalism, privatization seemed to promise an end to the inefficiencies of central planning—the key to freeing the resources and talents of this huge area and lifting its living standards to those of the industrial countries.

What broad lessons were learned from the experience of the past 10 years? An unprecedented transformation has already occurred as these countries have moved from central planning in the direction of more competitive, market-oriented economies. Along with their successes, prominent failures have also marked this recent history, especially in Russia and in other countries of the former Soviet Union. The overall task ahead thus remains vast if the original vision of greater freedom and higher living standards is to be realized.

First, a little background. Ten years ago analysts said there was no theory to guide the practical process of transition, only theories of capitalism and socialism. This may still be true in the sense that a new consensus is only beginning to emerge, but it is not that difficult to cobble together a workable "model" of transition or transformation. Two key changes needed are *forcing a move from a sellers' to a buyers' market* (through price liberalization) and *enforcing a hard budget constraint* (through privatization and eliminating various government support mechanisms). These are the two principal incentives for profit-maximizing market behavior by all economic agents. Economists add to these two other elements at the core of change: *reallocating resources from old to new activities* (through closures and bankruptcies combined with establishing new enterprises) and *restructuring within surviving firms* (through labor rationalization, product line change, and new investment).

Combined, the resulting new incentives lead to dynamic movements reminiscent of the kind of "creative destruction" by entrepreneurial activity envisioned by the late economist Joseph A. Schumpeter, only with a much larger impact than Schumpeter's model envisioned. This general framework for transition has, at its center, *enterprises* as the key agents of change, just as the early writings presaged. However, it is less this theory and more the history of market economies that led to the view that *private* enterprises play the key role.

Better understanding of what has been achieved so far in Eastern and Central Europe should smooth and speed the big changes that still must come. After a decade of transition experience in the post-socialist camp, what can now be said about the expected central role of privatization in the process? A review of the large and growing research on privatization* suggests an analytical framework consisting of five themes:

- *Labors of Hercules:* The size of the task is vast, and incomparably larger than any previous privatization efforts. Can it be done reasonably quickly—that is, in a decade or two?
- *The Bottom Line of Efficiency Gains:* Is some privatization better than none, or more better than less? Can privatization be carried out as an isolated process, or does the government first have to prepare the playing field? Does speedy privatization work better than a slow, deliberate approach?

---

*Note: Citations for the studies on which this paper is based may be found in IMF Working Paper 99/6, "Privatization in Transition Countries: A Sampling of the Literature," by Oleh Havrylyshyn and Donal McGettigan.

- *The Agency Problem (Methods of Privatization):* Since owners are not in most cases able to be managers as well, the manager-agent's motivation may be a problem. Do some forms of privatization address the agency problem better than others?
- *The Dinosaurs versus Greenfields Choice:* After a decade of experience, analysts now see that start-up or greenfield enterprises are an important alternative, or additional, path for increasing private sector activity. The question then arises, what is the relative importance of privatization versus the importance of businesses begun from scratch? Can dinosaurs learn new tricks once they are privatized, or is it better to let them die a slow death while relying on start-ups to build the private sector? Are there trade-offs between the two?
- *Blind Justice of Market Competition:* In both the theory and practice of market economies, the advantage of private ownership stems from its profit-maximizing behavior conditioned by a competitive market environment. Can the essentials of a competitive environment be identified, providing a level playing field for all enterprises, whether start-ups, newly privatized, or still state-run?

Although definitive conclusions on these important issues are probably still years away, consensus is forming on some of the key findings, and early indications are emerging on a number of others.

Labors of Hercules

The ownership structure of the Eastern and Central European economies has changed rapidly and significantly since their independence. The magnitude of privatization already achieved is unprecedented, with hundreds of thousands of small firms and service establishments, and perhaps 60,000 medium- and large-scale operations, privatized in less than a decade. That is nearly 10 times the number of privatizations in the rest of the world in the previous 10 years or so.

The numbers of new private companies started in the former socialist world are similarly unprecedented. New firms numbered in the hundreds of thousands for the large countries in transition, and in the millions for the entire group of 25 or so non-Asian transition economies. The proportion of the output of these countries produced by start-up companies is substantially higher for Central Europe and the Baltics than for the countries of the Commonwealth of Independent States. But even the latter averages are surprisingly high.

While the private sector expanded quite rapidly in most transition countries, some countries—such as Belarus and Turkmenistan—remain exceptions, according to figures compiled by the World Bank and the European Bank for Reconstruction and Development (EBRD). By 1995, countries of Central Europe and the Baltics generally had far larger private sectors than most countries of the former Soviet Union (except Russia), but by 1997 the gap had narrowed considerably.

In most transition economies, however, a high proportion of economic activity remains in state hands. For example, one of the most advanced countries in private sector development, the Czech Republic, still holds all or a majority stake in the major utilities, majority ownership in 40 large firms and banks considered strategic, as well as the majority share in 30 nonstrategic firms.

Although the privatization yet to be accomplished is huge, commitment to reform remains strong and widespread in most countries. This suggests that the privatization still needed can probably be undertaken in the next decade or so.

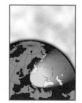

Bottom Line of Efficiency Gains

The evidence so far is unequivocal that some privatization in any form is better than none. To those guided by the early evidence from Poland, that may be surprising. Poland's early progress showed that state enterprises could raise efficiency quite quickly, and this encouraged the idea that efficiency could be achieved by state industries without privatization. But investigation shows that Polish managers of state firms performed well because they expected privatization and hoped their achievements would assure their survival when it came.

Since that early Polish experience, numerous studies in other countries have shown that privatized firms outperform comparable state enterprises almost invariably. For example, a study of several thousand privatized firms in seven Eastern European countries shows that they average annual productivity growth of 4–5 percent, five times the rate for state-owned enterprises, even when one controls for the degree of bank lending, subsidies, and other country-specific conditions. Privatized firms reduced their labor force by 20 percent more than comparable state-owned firms and ceased to receive direct government subsidies. Many studies also found strong evidence of positive effects of private ownership on several measures of enterprise performance.

While the conclusion is clear that privatization is necessary, the above results do not assure that all privatizations produce equal efficiency gains. Although it is early to reach a definite conclusion, the empirical analysis and quantitative assessments of experience so far do suggest that the form of privatization does matter, as do the pressures of competition and market environment.

On speed, the hypothesis "'Tis better 'twere done quickly" remains unverified and indeed virtually unresearched. Students of the problem are tempted by the comparisons of three cases: Poland (slow but deliberate progress), and Russia and the Czech Republic (speedy). The former appears to be far more successful, and the latter somewhat less successful; Russia dramatically less so. But two difficulties preclude a clear conclusion. Most other countries are in the slower group; their success is decidedly mixed. Moreover, Hungary, Estonia, and Latvia made fast and successful progress. Also, the other conditioning factors in these cases vary a great deal.

Nonetheless, in the recent revisionist view, policymakers fear that speedy privatization risks incorrect implementation, with inadequate development of supporting institutions and the danger that the whole process is taken over by antireform interests primarily seeking government favors. That this has happened can be demonstrated; that it was inevitable cannot. But perhaps, to noneconomists (certainly historians), this is all moot. At the pace of privatization seen since 1989, it will be almost complete for most of these countries in another decade, and twenty years for such a large task will be judged to have been very quick indeed.

The Agency Problem

The method of privatization (see Box) does seem to matter a great deal in explaining efficiency improvements, confirming the concerns of those that emphasized early on the agency problem: the well-known concern that non-owner managers do not have the same profit motive as owners and are unlikely to operate in the most efficient way assumed in theory. Long documented in industrial countries, the agency problem is seen anew in various ways in the many countries in transition from central planning to competitive markets. Although the evidence is far from clear, the empirical literature does reveal an approximate ordering of superiority. Start-up firms are clearly the best performers, showing the greatest efficiency gains; firms dominated by outsiders, especially with foreign investors involved, generally show good improvement; insider-dominated firms are the least efficient among the newly privatized, with an

Pros and Cons of Different Privatization Methods

Restitution. Restitution tries to return state assets to their former private owners in situations where the government's original acquisition is seen as unjust, such as uncompensated seizure. Redressing the worst examples of past injustices, it is argued, is essential on moral grounds.

Opponents of restitution counter that the process is necessarily selective, and therefore an unsatisfactory way of achieving justice retroactively. As a practical matter, private claims can often be complicated and drawn out, bogging down privatization unnecessarily. In practice, the transition countries have seldom used restitution, except for Estonia and, to a lesser extent, the Czech Republic.

Direct Sales and Equity Offerings. In the early 1990s, many of the former socialist countries planned to privatize through direct sales, emulating successes elsewhere, such as in the United Kingdom and Chile. At first some of them pursued this approach vigorously, but political and practical drawbacks quickly emerged. Ultimately East Germany, Estonia, Hungary, and to a lesser extent Poland were among the few successful users of this approach.

The initial goal was to sell state assets to outside investors in view of the underdeveloped state of domestic capital markets. Policymakers expected three gains: revenue earnings for the state, the rapid infusion of outside expertise, and the likelihood that management by outside owners would be more effective.

Among the practical drawbacks, the inadequacy of national stock markets and the lack of domestic capital proved to be greater handicaps than expected, and foreign investors, unable to obtain sound information on the enterprises offered, lacked sufficient interest. Furthermore, the direct sales approach was costly and slow, owing to the complexity of preparing each state asset for sale individually, and then ensuring that buyers lived up to contract provisions.

Politically, direct sales and equity offerings could be stalled when the general public saw the process as unfair. Powerful local interests, such as workers and managers, sometimes blocked consideration of direct sale privatizations. *(continued)*

Pros and Cons (concluded)

Management-Employee Buyouts. Under this approach, shares of an enterprise are sold or given to some combination of managers and other employees. The powerful positions of employees—as, for example, in Poland, and of managers, as in Russia—give this approach the twin advantages of feasibility and political popularity. It is also rapid and easy to implement. Well-structured management-employee buyouts can sometimes lead to efficient results, since they align the incentives of workers and owners.

Nevertheless, experience shows that these buyouts suffer serious disadvantages. Yielding to insider interests often entails large costs in inefficiency and poor management. The process may be inequitable, handing employees, rather than the population at large, most of the benefits. The record of labor-managed firms suggests that they may grant excessive wage increases, maintain excessively high employment, and undertake insufficient investment. In the transitional economies, insiders may also lack many of the skills necessary to function in a market-oriented economy.

Despite its many disadvantages, management-employee buyouts have been popular in several transition countries, including Croatia, the former Yugoslav Republic of Macedonia, Poland, Romania, the Slovak Republic, Slovenia, and Russia.

Mass Privatization. In mass, or equal-access, voucher privatization, the government generally gives away, or sells for a nominal fee, vouchers that can be used to purchase shares in enterprises. This technique was rarely used elsewhere in the world before the massive transition started in Central and Eastern Europe, but it has proved

unclear distinction between the management-dominated and the worker-dominated cases; the least efficient of all are the remaining state-owned enterprises.

In addition, the method of privatization appears to matter a great deal in a way not foreseen earlier: some forms of insider-dominated privatization may generate oligopolistic vested interests that will work against the establishment of an open, competitive environ-

popular there, particularly in the Czech Republic, but also in Armenia, Kazakhstan, the Kyrgyz Republic, Latvia, and Lithuania.

Voucher privatization helps to overcome the shortage of domestic capital. At the outset of transition, voucher schemes were politically popular because they addressed the perceived unfairness of other approaches and avoided the charges of a sellout of national assets to foreigners. The difficulties associated with valuing enterprises before privatization are also avoided.

As the name implies, mass privatization is a quick, simple way of completing large, economy-wide privatization programs—just what the transition economies needed. Early proponents argued that the fast pace of voucher privatization would add to the credibility of reform programs and bolster their chance of success. At times, the speed could prevent employees or other interests from mobilizing opposition to privatization. Furthermore, the widespread participation of a country's citizens fosters a greater understanding of reform and creates a new owner class with a stake in the process.

Mass privatization has its downside, however. The main risk is that a dispersed ownership structure will lack the focus and power to direct effective corporate management. This, in turn, may scare off potential new sources of capital. In practice, these problems have been partly addressed by pooling ownership interests in investment or mutual funds. The funds, however, do not always have adequate management, control, and supervisory powers, and managements can and do deprive them of essential information. In such cases, voucher privatization becomes merely ineffective absentee ownership.

ment, and against providing a level playing field for start-up entrepreneurial activity. With government privileges added (most commonly so far in the form of tax exemptions), the result is a continuation of a soft budget and a distorted allocation of resources toward the less efficient and the politically favored.

Furthermore, in practice the design of privatization programs in transition economies is largely dictated by political rather than economic conditions. At the start of transition, because the state held most assets, private wealth for buying them was inadequate. This led to the prospect of giveaways of state assets to a tiny segment of the population (or foreign buyers)—a politically infeasible course of action in many countries. By contrast, because mass privatization allowed a much greater participation by the general population, it was more politically acceptable. Ironically, in some cases, such as in Russia and Ukraine, mass privatization designed to prevent asset concentration in fact may have enhanced it.

The Dinosaurs vs. Greenfields Choice

On the question of whether it is possible to expect old dinosaurs to learn new profit-maximizing tricks after privatization, or whether it is better to give up on them, the evidence suggests that a combined approach may be best. Start-up or greenfield activity has been very important in expanding the size of the private sector and also in achieving efficiency gains in the economy. Research shows start-up firms are overwhelmingly most efficient and superior to even the best privatized firms. But the ordering of privatization forms noted above also means that some dinosaurs can learn new tricks and not all should be dismissed as hopeless.

An equally important conclusion is how the presence of start-up firms contributes to the appropriate competitive environment and puts pressure on newly privatized firms of all types to achieve comparable efficiency. Of course, these results rely on "ease of entry" to permit start-up firms to be set up and thrive. Some analyses also show that new firms are a main source of economic growth. In Poland, for example, small and medium-sized enterprises played a far more important role in the move toward a market economy than the privatization program, which lagged behind other economic reforms. One study of Russia concludes that governments should concentrate more on the development of small and medium-size enterprises than on privatization itself.

Blind Justice of Market Competition

Which is more important, setting up a well-designed privatization program, or creating a supportive market environment? It is tempting to conclude that the general market environment is much more important than the method of privatization. Eventually, evidence may support this view, but so far almost no empirical privatization studies have taken account of such variables as degree of competition, rule of law, and other institutional factors, and therefore no such conclusion is warranted.

Nevertheless, two impressions so far argue for the importance of the market environment. One is that start-up firms, which clearly face the forces of competition, outperform all others no matter what privatization method is used. The other is that private sector development in Central Europe, partly because of its better property rights environment, is more successful than in the former Soviet Union.

If these ideas are to be credited, the backdrop against which privatization efforts have taken place is important. And what is known about supportive market environments suggests that four elements are essential: macroeconomic stability, hard budget constraints, competitive markets, and adequate property rights.

Macroeconomic Stability. High and variable inflation is widely known to harm an economy's growth prospects. The difficulties of operating in an uncertain environment shorten business decision horizons and negatively affect the private sector. High inflation usually brings high nominal and real interest rates and adds to the costs of private sector investment. It is also likely to be accompanied by macroeconomic instability in other areas, for example, reflecting an underlying fiscal profligacy likely to engender uncertainty among private sector participants. Exchange rate depreciation and volatility also typically accompany high inflation, adding uncertainty to international trading arrangements and financing.

Hard Budget Constraints. Government subsidies that prop up inefficient loss-making firms include direct budget subsidies; soft credit from the state, banks, or other institutions; a toleration of persistent arrears among related enterprises and in tax and energy payments; and selective tax cuts for weak firms.

A hard budget constraint forces enterprises to be more aggressive in collecting receivables, linking investment more closely to profitability, and shifting objectives from simply meeting output targets to making profits. A radically different approach to economic policy is required for transition countries to eradicate soft budget constraints. Government commitments to programs supported by international organizations, such as the IMF, can help them resist the temptation to prop up failing companies.

Competitive Markets. Many studies now confirm the positive role of increased competition in raising enterprise performance. An end to permissive government support to enterprises is an essential step toward competitive markets and helps force firms to concentrate on price, quality, variety, and customer service. An end to central planning and price controls, and openness to imports, add competitive pressure as transition progresses. Finally, a competitive labor market is important, in place of the tightly controlled, paternalistic labor markets that prevailed under central planning.

Property Rights. Owners must be assured of the right to use assets, to decide on their use by others, and to profit from their use and sale. Progress has been made in the legal area of property rights. But researchers identify a variety of weaknesses that transition countries, even the more advanced, must address to protect property rights adequately, including stronger civil codes and more efficient court proceedings on property rights. On bankruptcy and liquidation procedures, continuing problems include uncertain values resulting from restitution claims, problems with seizure and resale, and a weak judicial system.

Summary and Conclusions

Two clear lessons emerge from the literature. Private enterprises almost invariably outperform state-run companies. In other words, any privatization is better than none, regardless of whether a stable, competitive environment has been established first or not.

A second, surprising, lesson: private companies started from scratch rank as the best performers, followed by newly privatized firms run by outsiders, either local or foreign. Privatized companies dominated by insiders are least efficient and productive, but even these regularly do better than state enterprises. Researchers have not yet charted the full implications of the vital role of start-up firms. But these firms' vigor and their contributions to economic growth, as well as to fostering competitive systems, raise new issues that may influence the future of reform efforts.

If a country is to foster sustainable private sector development—whether through a well-designed privatization program or start-ups—it must ensure that an appropriate market environment is in place. Soft budget constraints—continued direct subsidies, imprudent bank lending, and write-offs of bad debt by the government—retard enterprise restructuring; managers may spend more time lobbying the government for support than undertaking painful restructuring measures. A significant complementary aspect is how much competition enterprises face.

It is tempting to conclude that the general market and competitive environment is more important than the method of privatization. Eventually, evidence may support this, but the research so far does not permit such a conclusion. Two findings argue in favor of it: start-up firms outperform others no matter what privatization method is used, and the success of Central European private sector development relative to the former Soviet Union countries partly reflects a better property rights business environment. But these "facts" are impressionistic; to date almost no empirical studies have controlled for market environment, degree of competition, rule of law, and other institutional factors.

Perhaps the most important lesson after a decade of transition in the centrally planned economies to market-oriented systems is that private sector development can surely be rated a success. Despite a handful of reversals as well as slowdown in 1998, most transition countries are now recording positive growth in output—the bottom line indicator of trends in efficiency.

The Economic Issues Series

1. *Growth in East Asia: What We Can and What We Cannot Infer.* Michael Sarel. 1996.

2. *Does the Exchange Rate Regime Matter for Inflation and Growth?* Atish R. Ghosh, Anne-Marie Gulde, Jonathan D. Ostry, and Holger Wolf. 1996.

3. *Confronting Budget Deficits.* 1996.

4. *Fiscal Reforms That Work.* C. John McDermott and Robert F. Wescott. 1996.

5. *Transformations to Open Market Operations: Developing Economies and Emerging Markets.* Stephen H. Axilrod. 1996.

6. *Why Worry About Corruption?* Paolo Mauro. 1997.

7. *Sterilizing Capital Inflows.* Jang-Yung Lee. 1997.

8. *Why Is China Growing So Fast?* Zuliu Hu and Mohsin S. Khan. 1997.

9. *Protecting Bank Deposits.* Gillian G. Garcia. 1997.

10. *Deindustrialization—Its Causes and Implications.* Robert Rowthorn and Ramana Ramaswamy. 1997.

11. *Does Globalization Lower Wages and Export Jobs?* Matthew J. Slaughter and Phillip Swagel. 1997.

12. *Roads to Nowhere: How Corruption in Public Investment Hurts Growth.* Vito Tanzi and Hamid Davoodi. 1998.

13. *Fixed or Flexible? Getting the Exchange Rate Right in the 1990s.* Francesco Caramazza and Jahangir Aziz. 1998.

14. *Lessons from Systemic Bank Restructuring.* Claudia Dziobek and Ceyla Pazarbaşıoğlu. 1998.

15. *Inflation Targeting as a Framework for Monetary Policy.* Guy Debelle, Paul Masson, Miguel Savastano, and Sunil Sharma. 1998.

16. *Should Equity Be a Goal of Economic Policy?* IMF Fiscal Affairs Department. 1998.

17. *Liberalizing Capital Movements: Some Analytical Issues.* Barry Eichengreen, Michael Mussa, Giovanni Dell'Ariccia, Enrica Detragiache, Gian Maria Milesi-Ferretti, and Andrew Tweedie. 1999.

18. *Privatization in Transition Countries: Lessons of the First Decade.* Oleh Havrylyshyn and Donal McGettigan. 1999.